POETRY IS BLOOD

T0192992

ESSENTIAL POETS SERIES 257

**Canada Council
for the Arts**

**Conseil des Arts
du Canada**

**ONTARIO ARTS COUNCIL
CONSEIL DES ARTS DE L'ONTARIO**

an Ontario government agency
un organisme du gouvernement de l'Ont

Canadä

Guernica Editions Inc. acknowledges the support of the Canada Council
for the Arts and the Ontario Arts Council. The Ontario Arts Council
is an agency of the Government of Ontario.

We acknowledge the financial support of the Government of Canada.

KEITH GAREBIAN

POETRY IS BLOOD

GUERNICA
EDITIONS

TORONTO – BUFFALO – LANCASTER (U.K.)
2018

Elana Wolff, editor
Michael Mirolla, series editor
Cover and interior design: Errol F. Richardson
Cover image: Detail of a pastel design by Keith Garebian
Guernica Editions Inc.
1569 Heritage Way, Oakville, (ON), Canada L6M 2Z7
2250 Military Road, Tonawanda, N.Y. 14150-6000 U.S.A.
www.guernicaeditions.com

Distributors:
University of Toronto Press Distribution,
5201 Dufferin Street, Toronto (ON), Canada M3H 5T8
Gazelle Book Services, White Cross Mills
High Town, Lancaster LA1 4XS U.K.

First edition.
Printed in Canada.

Legal Deposit – First Quarter
Library of Congress Catalog Card Number: 2017960393
Library and Archives Canada Cataloguing in Publication
Garebian, Keith, 1943-, author
Poetry is blood / Keith Garebian.
(Essential poets series ; 257)
Poems.
ISBN 978-1-77183-279-3 (softcover)
I. Title. II. Series: Essential poets series ; 257

PS8563.A645P64 2018   C811'.54   C2017-907297-8

for Lucine Kasbarian and Jirair Tutunjian
(my teachers in many things Armenian)

"a line of poetry's a line of blood"
—**Charles Wright**

CONTENTS

Part One: Old Griefs

Part Two: Disappearances

Part Three: Heartbeats And Footprints

Part Four: Meditations

PART ONE:
OLD GRIEFS

April

A month bequeathing poppies,
compact red explosions.

Insomniacs found bones
in meadows of ordinary light.

The Boy Watched

The boy watched dawn abdicating,
dusk and night prevailing.

Parents moved in stealth,
as killers came like wolves
to tear fresh flesh.

No hero to stop the quaking,
sadness of cold kilns, mildewing lavash.
Bones and need together,
no ark on water or land.

Dry-tongued, dry-eyed,
fire in the larynx,
part of him boiled away
to bigger infernos.

From that: much grief
and anger against a sky
of venomous sun, hawks
with razor-clam claws.

Old Griefs

His heavy body sagging at his middle daughter's coffin.
Dentures forgotten. Hollow cheeks.
She, named for his mother who died a drowned moon.
Oh, mother! he would groan amid some mental distress.
Oh, father, deaf to me on purpose.

Divided river, bizarre zodiac.
Tributaries of my blood from two directions:
the first, a many-fabled city suckling at the teat of Mother
          India;
the second, an ever-returning nightmare—
cauchemar, Armenia.

Wedding portrait of my parents:
a bouquet of bitter orange-blossom,
pool of white-water train.
He holds his breath and faces the camera
squarely. The moon a mirrored tangle of exiled shadows.

He, Adam, sinned against. An orphanage
with cousin Bedros;
freedom in their brown eyes, they sailed in a makeshift raft,
got caught. Armenian Tom and Huck,
the curved horizon

bending away. Adult in Bombay,
The Retreat, a mythic address,
a haunted home
dusted with regrets
how many kisses crushed

my parents, misfits suffering love.
Mother, soft and hidden within.
Father, hard and afflicted.
Canada our country by default, the icy shore.
A covert story under snow

and life thrashed up from childhood.
Stirred, like Raphael.
Old griefs, lucid reasons,
father implicit
in what I know:

an alphabet invented to keep a poetry to a people.
Most of a native language lost.
Stones stacked up by villagers to keep the earth strong.
A stone placed in the fork of a tree
could make a barren tree fruitful.

Certain stones brought milk to dried-up breasts.
Cutting off the head of a Turkish
corpse and throwing it into a river
brought rain—the peasants claimed.
My father had a different superstition:

His middle daughter's name meant gem.
When she became gravely ill,
he flung her pearl earrings away.
The land had strange fits.
Underground was close to hell.

Body could be a betrayal.
My father was always checking skin
and bowel. A survivor with a propensity for solutions.
He hoarded bulletins, magazines,
ties, socks, suits, shoes—

things he'd put to use in a far-off
time—a rope around his neck.
He knew of disappearances
and died alone and lonely,
mouth a gaping wound.

If I could touch his lips with words,
my fingertips would turn to gold from Horus.
He was a father and he was not,
in a time that was
and a time that wasn't.

Destroying Family Photos

Unsanctioned, my sister cast them away,
family photos, *memento mori*.
I could not measure the ratio
between her relief and my loss.

Pictures of childhood
smiles chiselled gems
carried into balmy youth
where love was intoxication.

Looking on faces, even of those
old and shuffling about,
opened the door to an exotic country
where parents fell in love
in quick time,
children believed
in sweet dreams and miracles.

Everything lived and bloomed,
life unrolled in stages,
fading sepia telling the story
of first love and the quiet
sadness of things.

Photos said more
than the roar or whisper
of words,
they caught the truth
of bindings and releases.

When everything dead is dead
and I have looked at my sister
with contempt
and released her from my violent feeling,
the ghosts of those photos
will lean towards me,
forgiving us both
for the brief world's work
of loading and unloading.

Okra

It's in the same family—
mallow, along with cotton, cocoa, hibiscus.

If I had known more about families,
I would have shared my father's love for okra.

It had strange origins, coming from Ethiopia.
Was used by Egyptians and Moors.
Its Igbo name is *Okum*.
Bamyah in Arabic. Lady's fingers in other zones.

Our family name is from Arabic. Gareb—
from the land of strangers. Or simply stranger.
Another story my father forgot to tell us
when he narrated his displacements.

From flowers four to eight centimetres in diameter,
with five white to yellow petals.
Often with a red or purple spot at the base of each.

Distinguishing marks. He didn't have any,
except his strong manual labour hands,
with thick fingers and machine oil under the nails.

Okra is pronounced only one way.
Not so our Armenian family name.
Some families hate the ambiguous.

He loved the fruit,

except none of us knew it as that.
It was vegetable. Two metres tall, with long, broad leaves
and capsules containing many white seeds.

Did he know the leaves were heart-shaped?
I was searching for his heart but he never knew.

I hated the mucilaginous thing
with its ridged skin,
a pod which oozed slime
when broken in stew. It went down
like medicine rather than fruit.

He liked it best in curry,
where it had new texture. Another story.

Why do you pick at it? he asked me,
querulous. I wanted to speak words
that were hurtful.
Nothing to do with okra.

A Bird Cries in an Orchard

A bird cries, its claws tangled in wires.
There is an orchard
where a bird is tangled in a place of fat fruit.

You can hear the cries from the hilltop.
There is a world
where cries are heard in hilltops and in orchards.

Sky exists for a bird and for cries.
Orchards exist for fat fruit.
A bird cries in an orchard.
I know why this is so.

As long as there is fruit there will be birds.
There are wires to keep the fruit clear.
So long as there are wires
there will be cries.

When the bird falls in an orchard
you can hear the cry.
Inside my memory, a cry.

Just as there is a cry inside my memory
so there is a fallen bird in an orchard of fat fruit.

You can see something dark
in an orchard from the hill tops.
The orchard, nothing but things torn,
cries of birds and fat fruit.

Inside the mind is an orchard,
in that orchard, a bird-cry
and wasted fruit.
The orchard is a wound.

There is an orchard without fat fruit,
fat fruit without an orchard in the mind.

The skin of the fruit is a thing to be torn
the cries of birds on a sunny day
inside the skin, the sound, the wound.
You are silent
before such things.

Errata

For "farm" read "harm."
For "code" read "goad."
For "lax" read "tax."
For "feast" read "beast."

For "odour" read "other."
For "vain" read "pain."
For "life" read "strife."
For "dessert" read "desert."

For "rope" read "rape."
For "dance" read "trance."
For "village" read "pillage."
For "disparate" read "desperate."

For "assimilate" read "assassinate."
For "horror" read "trauma."

Title Search

Genesis Angels. The Armenians in the Byzantine Empire.
The Historical Monuments of Nakhichevan. David of
      Sassoon.
The History of the Armenian People. The Kingdom of
      Armenia.
The Battle of the Prophets. Armenia:
A Rugged Land. Land of Fire.

When Darkness Falls Upon Us. Time of Your Life.
Massacres, Resistance, Protectors.
Forty Days of Musa Dagh. Armenian
Revolutionary Movement. Armenian Golgotha.
Earthquake. The Burning Tigris. Leavening the Levant.

Sad Days of Light. Children of Ararat.
Pogrom A Novel of Armenian History.
Exile in the Cradle. Black Dog of Fate.
Convent of Cypresses, A Hill of Bones.
Last Rites. Reservoir of Ancestors.

Words and Photographs.
Martyrdom and Rebirth. From the Book of One Thousand
      Tales.
Armenian Immigrants. Merchants from Ararat.
Rough Landing. Coming to Terms.
Armenian Songbook. The Legacy.

Pain: Journeys Around My Parents.
How to Choose Your Past. Chance Meetings.
Voyages. Madness in the Family.
A Brief History of Armenia.
Songs of Bread, Songs of Salt.

Wine for the Living. Sacred Wrath.
Armenia on the Road to Independence.
A Mandate for Armenia.
Passage to Ararat. Rise the Euphrates.
The Circle Dancers.

My Name is Aram. The Romantic.
O My Generation.
My Brother's Road.
The Human Comedy.
The Legacy of Lost Things.

PART TWO:
DISAPPEARANCES

Death by Drowning

Seven wave gravely at low tide
from a bank by the water,
escaping the slow
strangulation of liquid deep.

The dead's gurgling cries are sirens
in their ears,
and the minds of the seven
are caught

by young bodies going down
like premature suns, and the old
are ancient rays on the last shores
of days.

Those cries are lightning
in the bones of the seven,
more jagged than wailing
on the shores of the living.

Horizon electrified,
the seven cast diving-bell eyes
deep to the bone-orchard
where no sun can reach.

On the burning surface of shore,
the seven ache
in their bones, sea-gazing,
lonely in their thoughts
growing deeper than graves.

Deir ez-Zor

Rasping in the burning air,
their throats open graves,
more days and nights
in sands of hallucination.

Their broken bodies belong to silence,
their names kneel inside them,
begging mutely
in abandonment,
stop the slow extinguishing

the turning inside-out
of skin, hiding places,
burnt-out minds, heart,
the desperate questions:

Is there a better death?
Is there home awaiting?

Humanity sucked up,

never a sensible way to explain
the sudden cancelled world,
forced sadness of parting,

begetting nothing.

Even the sun sucked in.

Memorial

In July's white light
    a perfect harmony—
hill and arrow-shaped
    stela split vertically.

Violent crevice,
    violent as dispersion
as upheaval, seasons
    making a world of bones.

Ashes in glass casings, soil
    from tombs with great names—
legends of Wegner, Werfel,
    Lepsius, Bryce.

Ashes and glass, soil and tombs
    names that stay,
basalt mourning—
    grief of stone.

The wall speaks names
    of bodies unrisen
from faraway
    despoiled graves

we can enter.
    This is what the living do
to memorialize the names
    lifting us unroofed—

twelve tablets—inward leaning
    khatchkars carved with crosses
figures mourning, twelve
    lost provinces

holding restless heart
    and mind,
within the stony circle
    where the stairs

lead down to fire
    from sunken stone.
Raising spirits from sleep's
    rapt quiet.

Something snaps
    makes hot tears spurt,
yet there are no words
    to measure pathos.

What surfaces are sounds
    that claw the wretched
tones that break
    the throat.

This dirt we call earth,
    can you taste what I'm saying?
This requiem
    ill with carnage of a people.

Garni Temple

My hand could hurt
pressing it, ancient stone
exactingly hammered,
tested by sun's stroke
wind and rain's buffeting
snow's resentment.

It carries me back to dawns
when sea wrinkled first shores
when moon kissed early mountains
and many tongues
sent prayer and pleading
to awesome gods
of waxing danger.

This sculpted sanctuary,
proudly empty, gigantic enough
to darken the sky
with massive discipline
of labouring men, burdened
by sheer weight
of haunting silence.

Blind face turned
to Mithra, it is temple
upon Urartian temple,
grey basalt cellas
concealing revered deities,
stony Titan on square pedestals
straining to hold all on his shoulders.

At high noon, the sun-filled
space spills light
numbing my long gaze.
In migrant solitude, I stand,
noting the distant dry river
winding like a long dissembling worm.

Pilgrims move as on a drugged path,
fervent hearts pulsing
in wind-stilled hush
of pillars, pediments, and altars,
the gods withdrawn, mute as urns.

The Walls of Diyarbekir

Old walls, volcanic rock.
A shape of containment,
relics and small lives
cloistered in silence.
Rock by black rock, they lived in this place
closed in. Old walls infested
with snakes, scorpions,
spider webs.

Always hard
not to have a safe place,
to feel cut off
because your spire, Sourp Giragos,
stands taller than a minaret.

A foreign people, these ancestors.
But they have something to tell me.
They can't name all
that was destroyed of their race.

Stonework of penetrable dreams.

Stone, metal, spirit
locked in spirals
diminishing together.
On this side of silence
there are no smiles.

Yet we must dream above
the fallen bell-tower,
the eight-sided clock,
bell cast in Istanbul.
Dream of poems in these walls
where one sad person talked to another,
songs surging out of souls
singing to the moon
after slow sunsets.

A True Portrait of Talaat Pasha

Would you like it? Would you like it if I told?
Would you like it if I told you about the end?
The end if I told you.
Would you like it?
If I at the end told.
You would like it?
Would you like the end be told?
If I would.
What do you want?
You want it now?
Now.
And now.
Now exactly as I told.
An end must be put.
Exactly an end.
However you want.
As I told you.
Settled the question settles exactly settles with no regard.
Settles either age or sex or scruples do not regard.
Now exactly repeat with no regard. Age sex scruples.
No regard. Exactly. Repeat. No regard.
What do you want? You want what? Would you like the end
be told exactly? Would you like it?
You want it now?
It is settled.
No more. There are no more.
Armenians.
There are no more.
Armenians.

There are no more Armenians.
There are no more Armenians.
There are no more Armenians.
As I told you. Exactly.
Repeat exactly.
As I told you. Repeat.
Exactly as I told you.
An end.
As I told you.
Exactly.
With no regard.

Genocide Paintings

Bludgeoned flesh
abandons the bone house,
structured self.
Tattered cotton slanders skin,
nakedness is sacramental.

Desolation is requiem,
violence an *étude*.

We no longer count
stars and their celestial warnings,
no longer expect purification
of a defiled history.

We shake fists, utter stories
on slippery slopes,
are moved.

We have waited more than a century
burning prayers, laying fruit
on grieving altars
as earth falls deeper into wretchedness.

We see beyond seeing,
each painting a spectre,
a memory staggering
from Armenia in dying breaths,
tears flooding the waters
of Lake Van.

Siamanto's Dismay

Caught in the world's toils,
emptiness in heart
filling us, we measure
stagger and silence,

measure coffins of sunset
slur of landscape
final vocabularies
of little mortality.

We cannot see beyond seeing,
burning fields, cauldron caves,
corpse-engorged rivers.
Nothing to make it otherwise.

We learned to dance in flame
at the urging of frantic whips,
strangle our outcries,
fall into a black hole of history.

Black dog of fate
hounding us to hell,
its heart colder than its eyes.
we learned

how to live for the last time,
taking blood-red pomegranates
to heart and mind,
remembering what

we never could say
of sleepless fish,
locust pods, last leaves,
live coals on our tongues.

Siamanto's Grief

Grief is a homeless dog
slavering over a meatless bone.

Grief invades the darkness of ditches
where the homeless huddle.

Grief is April rain spitting on skinned corpses,
spring of somnolent ashes.

Grief is a sky of falling stars
smashing church steeples.

Spits on justice
after the piling of bones
in seizures of autumn.

Your grief was ecstasy
in blazes of poetry
lighting up a lowering sky.

The Unnamed are Nothing

Elegy for ordinary people
many cut short in daylight
multa lux
or late at night
multa nox
this elegy is light and dark
drifting unalterable
across history
(often liquid)
flowing and questioning
dimensions, weights,
locations, moods, names,
even smells. For death
is odoriferous: we die and smell
like dead dogs or maggots.

We need elegies, need history
for the asking
as at Exampaios
where a population was reduced
to melted arrowheads in a bowl.
That bowl leaves memory
of a number, and that number
knows the truth,
as the sea laughs at us in waves
and the sky rains down mockery.

My father's people vanished into nothing
and I reach into the corners of night
to guess where their spirits may pass.
Clues are laconic, do not grow
names of the dead.
I am made sadder by night
for there is no centre to his mystery,
no key to unlock his oblivion.

Yet there is a closeness with these dead
and an extravagance, my displacement
out of their time and space.
I consign myself to night
and the collective dead
who remain unnamed
and therefore nothing.
Nothing is night's gift.

PART THREE:
HEARTBEATS AND FOOTPRINTS

Komitas

April is the month
of cut flowers,
sun a scimitar
tumbling us down.

Butterflies
over poppies
glisten by roads of blood
in the wrong place.

Stuttering genius,
sombre cypresses
green cones
thrusting to clouds.

Trees are bandits
lying in ambush.
He cowers under
tables and garment hems.

They will come, he is certain,
the armed police.
He will never stand
in sun-light again.

Stalking shadows—
everything comes from something.
Even clouds cast shadows,
keep us from the light.

He longs for silence,
counts syllables
in church caves, weighted
by darkness,

lives more secretly than ever,
lantern in his mind,
lips sounding
a son-to-mother lullaby,

his dark prelate's robe flapping
to the whip of wind. He writes
a dangerous song of black wings
rustling in the tree of twisted self.

Songs of Nagash the Ghareeb

Shape-shifter, castaway,
sometimes a ghost to himself.

He cannot know the map of earth,
only his own shadow across it.

Longing in his knapsack,
Rootlessness sewn into his shoes.

Skin sticky with memory
Invisibly splintered.

How long, how long
the song of exile leaping from his mouth?

Tell Me Why

Tell me why you are drawn to sad music,
old dull pains, scars that linger generations.
Why your sleep is a struggle deep in a cave.

Tell me why history gives small hope,
why you need to live your life in ongoing battle.
Why your children must be part of your tale.

Cross it out.
It won't be the first cancellation.

Happiness is only brief.
Stumbling under black skies.
Short prickly star-shine.

This life is no city on a sacred hill.
We are difficult to one another
and love streams all the wrong ways.

Cross it out.
It won't be the first cancellation.

Tell me why cruelty gets in the way of love,
like wind knocking the heads off flowers,
like time bruising your shattered heart.

Tell me why your moments of tender mercy
are a mysterious penance.
Why this should really matter.

Cross them out.
It won't be the first cancellation.

Tell me why your name means stranger.
Always called behind your back.
Sets the world against you.

Tell me if your name makes you shiver,
if it turns your blood,
if it is forgotten.

It names my strange sad pain
that nothing takes away,
nothing can cancel out.

They Had Some Rugs

They had some rugs.

They had rugs that danced with children.
They had rugs that thought they were does.
They had rugs that made soft melodies.
They had rugs that wed sweet flutes.
They had rugs that sang with minstrels.
They had rugs that brought bright news.

They had some rugs.

They had rugs the colour of grapes.
They had rugs that soaked up laughter.
They had rugs that drowned in brandy.
They had rugs that warmed by the fire.
They had rugs that were proud of their place.

They had some rugs.

They had rugs that were magnifying glasses.
They had rugs that whispered at night.
They had rugs that lied to the household.
They had rugs that kept to themselves.

They had some rugs.

They had rugs that were shattered tufa.
They had rugs that were stained by rape.
They had rugs that cried at the moon.
They had rugs with eyes of oxen.

They had some rugs.

They had rugs that licked on sand.
They had rugs that were maps which could tear.
They had rugs that were membranes of oceans.
They had rugs that were madder than red.
They had rugs afraid of their names.

They had some rugs.

They had rugs they loved like their children.
They had rugs that prayed to the future.
They had rugs that faded like ink.
They had rugs they lost with their homelands.

They had some rugs.

Custodian

Ararat watches quietly,
touched by snow at its peaks.

April is here briefly,
a vigil light that goes out.

Centenary of slaughter
in a silence of God.
There is no need to imagine
a worse world.

And yet poppies bloom,
butterflies flit in orchards,
crowds mingle in Republic Square
couples stroll in Lover's Park.

And now, in a new April,
I peel off the shadows
in a massive landscape,

reborn in the stone geometry
of Garni Temple, blessed by spring water
from black rock of Geghard Monastery,
climb the white stairs
of the Cascades, linking Yerevan
to the war monument at the top.

The ardour of variegated things—
some hectic with tarnish,
aura of common objects,
forms of amberless dreaming.

I am their custodian
in poetry, climbing many stairs,
risking vertigo in search of stories,
my hands and mouth
the shape of an ark.

A Pilgrimage

My mind on its daily rounds
knows the centre is not always certain,
the moment rarely malleable
as my heart in its hunger
clings
to angular pictures
of stone walls on living rock,
swallow-tailed carvings,
cone-shaped mountain with its icy crest.
Garni temple aiming at the sun,
basalt porticos, Lion Head water spouts,
mosaic floors, decaying steam rooms,
stone floors broken by seismic eruptions—
a future manacled to past
as old as Babylon and Rome.

Terraced vineyards on stony hills
cannot hide a flawed fate:
The prime element is stone, not soil,
native stone, not native soil,
open-air museum of marble, granite,
pumice and tufa.
So many hearts locked inside stone,
if I touch the rock,
I feel these hearts
in a hard country blooming with royal skulls,
sad cavities where old songs fester
close to the barbwire border.

Ararat in the background
stands in chains.

History towers above mineral springs
bubbling in turquoise sunrise
over pink flamingos and pelicans.
As the moon hatches pale light,
deep silence shrouds my musing.
There are lessons to be learned
from listening to stone,
for the wordless can be brooding
speech, unsung yet undying.

Flesh has become grass, hearts
fused to mountain.
Our footprints
speech trailing
off like autumn, assertions
falling like gold leaves.
Wind flutes its way
past plums and vines,
cranes fly in long wings
against broad horizon.
Blue light descends
into ash-black
shadow over stone and soil.

I walk in my orphaned
father's shoes, their footfall
imprinting his voicelessness.
Words between us were
silence disguised, setting
us adrift on a flood
up the mountain.
Footprints are dust, speech
vanished, the heart
broken, knowing only
it will reach somehow
the always white
again,
visible and audible
in its high parched ache.

Strambotto

From my frosted window, the view is the same:
icy grey-blue lake water both old and young,
end of winter presaged in sun's red flame.
Still, the landscape does not mourn in nature's tongue,
changing with inclement weather, the hard heart's shame
in those who know where old bitter truths are hung,
shadows of strange fruit on ghostly trees claiming
the past a worthless instrument come unstrung.

Antitheses

One names a disease;
        the other refuses to be it.
One invents darkness;
        the other adds to light.
One sees the sickle moon as weapon;
        the other a mirror of doom.
One fabricates a net to stifle prey;
        the other is trussed up, a fatal goat.
One is an animal from the left side;
        the other a breathing ghost.
One laments the loss of ancient glory;
        the other mourns the barely born.
One prays in earnest after murdering;
        the other suffers noisy silence.
One feasts lasciviously in an old world;
        the other survives ugly meanings.
One lies to guard a nation's best-kept secret;
        the other rouses the revelation.
One clatters the crucifix to the ground;
        the other raises its perverse god again.

Sheep in Sun

Rocks clambering into russet,
the sturdy herder, staff in hand,
keeps close watch

of her wool-tufted
charges tugging dry grass.
Small black hooves, busy bells.

The afternoon blinks
cloudless in noon glare,
sun's blade cutting into the living.

Bleats and blares.
Far fields
glimmer to sheep eyes.

Slow white swaddling,
they let the tourist bus
pass, their beaded gaze,

dark tongues snagging
my attention, world outside the glass
bleating, breathing,
cut off.

I'm no keeper of sheep,
nor is my soul a shepherd
of seasons, observing
and following

still. A sadness like sunset
falls on me
after the clanging bells.
Wanderer, a stranger
in any land.

Wolves

First the eyes' heat
in fever of a dream,
wild loping gait,
ravenous snuffle.

They live as always
dragging meat—
long leashes of hunger
dripping blood.

Resist, and they tear you down,
fatten on a windpipe
or lung, snapping bone,
tearing off an arm.

Such hunger clamps mouths
on moon and sun,
appetites frenzy,
a murder song.

They feed their might
on a million ghosts.

The great emptiness
baying, gleaming in darkness.
Their brains never learn
why they live like this.

The Rivers

Chance casts its shadow
on bodies in the rivers,

water bloating bodies,
currents grinding,
aqueous graveyards,
                  swilling
rotting flesh from a gaping mouth.
Wedged between rocks,
corpses wait for fish.
The water washes them bare,
suspends them momentarily,
sweeps them into its surge.

Rivers from the east,
once copper-laden,
immanently divine:
Euphrates, now freighted
with the dead of Hayastan.
Tigris, swift river
south from the mountains, host
to capital and port.

You both have lost
divinity, become dumps
for human freight,
their presences
haunt the water,
float shadows,
residue of pain,
ever at risk of sinking.

Indestructible sand.
Rivers in the throat of time,
choked with wasted bodies,
raise ghosts
to extravagance of wind.
What do maps say of your water tongue?

At low tide,
departed selves
sway like underwater weeds.
All their stories in you.

PART FOUR: MEDITATIONS

My Father and I Rarely Touched

Yet something moved in secret, our roots deciding what forces to nurture.

We did not follow its motions.

His memories connected to hard things:

cracked earth, jagged rock, bones.

Names and faces evaporated.

Memories cut into time's dark glass—

a past in vanished shadows.

Photos of young Armenian orphans provoked my hunger for his boyhood face.

No photos of his family.

No photos of his birthplace.

His rages were dead photos,

the presence of absences.

Like the dark, we went on.

Despite the dark between us, I played in subtropical light.

A child's toy car. At the beach, my father's strong arms not quite grasping me in the surf. Posing with the family dog. Schoolboy pictures. My two younger sisters en route to Southampton. College photos, me in Shakespeare, Albee, and Wilde. Accusatory photos, failed marriages. Invisible photos, the heart trembling in fatherhood.

Adult photos could be ambiguous: with a bicycle, though I never knew him as a cyclist; with a lady on a dance floor, though he couldn't dance.
Sometimes presences add little detail.

Disappearances take it away.

Does light always fall at an angle coherent with thought?

If there's little light, do we know nothing or nothing well?

My father was often an image glimpsed, from the corner of my eye.

An apocalyptic flash.

The mind, like the eye, can bend light

behind surfaces, grow, looking within.

My mind attends to what vanished by crime.

An entire species of ghosts.

Landscape with nobody in it.

Archives of emptiness.

I root my father in an imagined place,

loved without judgement.

I give his ghost ascendancy. He will not be erased.

All blind spots gone, I imagine things differently.

This is the version I wish to tell.

Poetry is Blood

Time a winding sheet
stretched from century to century,
creased and blood-stained under sun
scald and biting wind; when winter
burns our shivering skin with cold.

The poem hones
hearts above a jagged abyss;
sings with bloody ecstatic lips,
holding feet to scarlet fire.

There will be no after-life
for anxiety, guilt, and shame—
only this message and melody:
the poem's lines a crimson pool
in memory of memory.

Finishing Sentences

Somewhere my body goes taut when

All history is burned out, down to

A slow, tortuous migration to the vanishing point on the
horizon line appears to be

Where a dense and baleful wind blows

There are blank sockets in place of eyes which once

Skeletons from another

Place and century, split and carved

Rooted in stone, gathering to itself

Their light hearts turned

Within us all, disasters are numb as

The baring of the stones

What drums in my bones

I feel the surging

I cannot forget the Golgotha we trod, century-old, and

The wolf's belly, the sheep's meekness

They climbing over the dead

Should we fling the bible away while we flap frantically in

A room from which it is always possible to view

Your life winding in me, while mine unwinds like

Spring awakening thoughts, spring poems are a condition of

The dialogue that lasts a lifetime is one which

After considering what was better, a world without
　　　　　Armenians or

The intentions of these words and poetry

It is one thing to insist like Adorno that there can be no
poetry after

Words and things can sometimes be

Language is, first of all,

Any theory of the self

Everything you hear in your head, heart, and body when you read this

By the very act of naming, one enters

There is no ladder but

Pull yourself up by the roots or

If your future has a history, then it is

Especially evident in the way of personal metaphor

My eyes are grooved with persuasions of

Shame, which is the spur for

The writer's rage to order words

I stand in the impudent ranks

Anything I say is as partial as

What was it like when

To the burning mouth,

No part was in touch with art,

Is not writing also part of

Our words for the dead, uttered in

A room where you are reading

After you've learned things, you're left

But we are the Mountain, so

A Biography of Deracination

All high mountains are dark coffins.

Ararat sometimes sighs.

The winds around Lake Van sing hysterically.

Memory speaks but is suspect.

The past sends me cards with words to assuage exile.

We always see the mountain on the side farthest from us.

Disappearance of roots from soil.

True description of deracination.

Historians, deep in dusty books, contemplate dispersion.

The concept of race murder and its denial.

Compulsory journeys overland or by sea.

Every story, a journey through a desert.

Or on water.

Its aftermath.

Sad eyes, deep-sea eyes.

Do you really look at them?

Names of pain, names forgotten and forbidden.

Delaying new catastrophe by reiteration.

I am driven by what some deny.

Myths are tricksters, like religions.

What is deferred?

I have often seen cranes;

never seen angels, dark or light.

Are there poems after the cries of ghosts?

One more tale to stay alive.

A language from a different century, the last one,

or the next.

A People No One Had Told You About

To discover a people no one had told you about
is to be troubled by their differences,
troubled by words in a different tongue.
They cannot tell us of their common days.

A stray dog laps water in a leaf-strewn stream.
Soon there will be blood in that water.
The mouth closes.

The black dog locks its gaze on mine.
The same creature lapped the blood-drunk river,
the same dog feasted on scraps.

The old father, to whom I was never close,
wanted his epitaph to read On the contrary.
This never came to pass.

The past is a strange beast.
That beast can die.
The die is cast.

This life we are supposed to love
till death.
Could we die at the height of beauty or strength?
We're on our knees in defeat.

Fear is the animal in hiding and trembling.
Fear comes with being in this world.

When God could not make us humble,
He made us humiliated,
naked,
unable to close the spaces,
huddling closer to zero than one another.

We look at clouds,
come face to face with their silence,
wonder
if we could stop God from existing,
would we?

Advent of another world
with no clear name,
one that won't deny its true name.

Only the Earth

So, parents and grandparents die and die
and we miss their ashes
as time moves to Debussy's music
under the sea.

We scour sands for secrets,
black scarves, broken relics.
The sky rapacious,
air incendiary,
weather confounds our
quest in the margins.

The dead are a mute veracity,
after-life hazard to deniers
who wish to kill
our grief,
quash facts,
pretending history is an erasable slate
on which nothing is written.

If we could believe
in a god who is true,
who does not truncate
our cries of rage;

if we could break this wall
obscuring barren apricot trees,
disarray of forms,
the never-brimming cup

buried in the definite desert,
we would float on auguries.

Settings can be bondage.

Ash, salt, sugar,
white tablecloths.
Fruit in glazed bowls.
Caged bird, bleeding pomegranates
on a chasm's edge.

The horizon is a ribbon of fire,
sunrise or sunset, a trophy.

Something shattered,
something erased,
something withstood.

Always we awake to burdens:
home a dead planet,
unpurged.
Our daily lives absent
of heavenly intervention.
A story without end.

Son of man,
there is only the earth.

Irreducible

The same crossing out of landscape,
    same slicing of bodies,
    skin petalling off bones.
    Same madness,
should you live long enough.

This is voice
for the bereaved—
lamentation moving like widows
whose deaths must be believed,
be meaningful.

What the terror of history
denies them.

Hysteria is narrative,
humming darkness.
Gloats itself into a whirlwind
of hands and weapons.
First comes pain,
which is to say worse
is yet to come—

days and nights with exit wounds,
outrage searing the mind,
revenge tumbling the heart,
loss of utter humanity.
How each of us becomes void.

Elegy

My father's ancient tribe writhes
on my written page,
groaning under a sullen sun
in a landscape of cadavers
so ghostly real
I can count their groans,
even in this harsh north
where introspection freezes
while birds flee on strong wings,
their cries waning in geometric wake.

I speak of myself when I speak of them,
my perennial hallucination
of death's pandemonium.
For I speak the word I hear in my flesh
from their flesh
and it is always unmitigated death.

But the poem lives,
is alive in sight as the word happens.
The dead, like the living,
tempt poetry
in an impromptu elegy,
insistent as breath.

Who sees them now,
sun-tormented, moon-misbegotten
carrion crew brought to a sudden stop.

Their wash hanging from trees,
plums and apricots,
pulp of pomegranates,
polished walnuts
pending hungry palms,
flowers in the yard
speaking in their own tongues,
cats in the doorway.

Children babbling at play,
grandparents sleeping defenceless,
mothers kneading dough
by passionate kilns.
Men working in humble rhythms,
their constant hands, steady as salt.
Youth in love with youth,
ardent in the furnace of desire,
flamed hearts
radiant from fire to fire.

There is no continuity
to ardour and such life
once the killing begins.
Time vanishing in black rage,
rooted in the heart's dark rancour.

No time for the dead
to go down
with warm remembrances.
No time for looking
at unbroken mountains,
the sky, the ground
tangent to wild red rivers.
No time to wait
for Jesus to arise from the crypt,
gather his sheep from slaughter.

I cannot refuse
their deaths, tattooed on the mind.
Noise grimaced,
their bones with the fish.

The earth moves on
and light dances
as I shelter the dead,
give them refuge in my words
so they may dream of themselves
preying on us as we once did on them.

Cranes

Sky shrinks as they ease down
to dark nests on rooftops,
air rippling with wingbeats.
Our eyes are sucked into
their settling, high-pitched,
relieved to return, ruffling.
Home again,
shadowed in the moment.

Cold wrapping itself around
feathers and nests,
air bluing toward night.
Something that doesn't need
to be imagined—
ritual of flight and return,
necessity and instinct quivering
faithfully. Look closely

for wide adjusting wings,
passive long legs
of centuries. The exiled
home without apology
to count last stars hovering
in the break of silence.

Monument

Black stone glinting in midday sun
has no face, no name. Split like a woman's belly
met by a bayonet, voiceless
but closer to me than women
who have come to remember the slashes
of vulture talons tearing at family corpses.

Continents away from the river
once black from swollen dead,
it is concerned with itself,
the names buried in its plinth.

It cannot reclaim, cannot uncoil
the talking whirlwind,
the sky plagued with locusts—
thick humming darkness.

What was human now stone,
something stared at.
There are no hands to cup the future,
no eye tilted at Ararat.

Fetish of Last Lines

The Legacy of Lost Things
in memory of memory,
no eye tilted at Ararat
in its high parched ache,
the gods withdrawn, mute as urns
with no regard.

After slow sunsets
and a time that wasn't,
growing deeper than graves,
live coals on our tongues
lighting up a lowering sky.
Nothing is night's gift.

Between unsaying and forgetting,
how each of us becomes void
in any land.
There is only the earth.

Notes

The epigraph is a quotation from "Disjecta Membra" in *Negative Blue* by Charles Wright.

"The Boy Watched": *lavash* is the name for a flat bread baked by Armenians in a kiln.

"Old Griefs": My father, Adam, was born in Dikranagerd (Diyabekir). He was only five years old at the time of the 1915 genocide. His middle daughter was named Elma, after his mother Almast (Armenian for "diamond") or Elmast (Turkish equivalent). *The Retreat* was the name of the compound in Bombay, where my family lived till 1961—the year of our immigration to Canada.

"Title Search" names full titles of actual books pertaining to Armenian history and culture.

"Death by Drowning" was inspired by an eye-witness account of Mrs. George Dar Arsanian, as quoted in "Saw Armenians Drowned in Groups," *New York Times*, 3 Feb., 1919.

"Deir ez-Zor": Deir ez-Zor is in the Syrian desert, and has been called the Auschwitz of the 1915 genocide.

"The Walls of Diyarbekir" makes reference to Sourp Giragos, the largest Armenian church in the Middle East, built in the 19th century and subjected to many cycles of destruction and rebuilding.

"A True Portrait of Talaat Pasha" is written in the manner of Gertrude Stein. Talaat Pasha (Mehmed Talaat) (1874-1921) was one of the infamous Three Pashas who were *de facto* rulers of the Ottoman Empire during the First World War. In response to the German ambassador who persistently brought up the Armenian question in 1918, he is claimed to have said: "What on earth do you want? The question is settled. There are no more Armenians." He was assassinated by a single bullet in Berlin by Soghomon Tehlirian, a member of the Armenian Revolutionary Federation. Tehlirian was acquitted of murder in the German court on grounds of temporary insanity owing to the trauma of the genocide.

"Siamanto's Dismay": Siamanto was Adom Yarjanian, born 1878 in Western Armenia, and was a newspaper editor, poet, and playwright. A master of free-verse narrative, he wrote about heroes who had shaped Armenian identity. Siamanto was murdered in Turkey in August, 1915.

"The Unnamed are Nothing": The final line is from Anne Carson's *Nox* (2010), a meditative elegy that inspired my poem.

"Komitas": Komitas (or Gomidas) (1869-1935) was born Soghomon Soghomonian. He was ordained as priest, and became a musicologist, composer, arranger, singer, choirmaster, and poet. Traumatized by the Armenian genocide, he devolved into paranoia, requiring treatment in various psychiatric hospitals in Paris, where he spent his last years in mental, physical, and spiritual agony. Nevertheless, he is celebrated as a pioneer of ethno-musicology, and one of the greatest of Armenian composers.

"Songs of Nagash the Ghareeb": Mkrtich Nagash (1390-1470) was born in Bitlis (North of Lake Van in the eastern part of present-day Turkey) to the family of a priest and educated in a variety of monastic schools, becoming a great scholar and high-ranking churchman. However, he ran afoul of the local Muslim authorities in Dikranagerd when he erected a church steeple taller than any of the neighbouring mosques, and was forced into exile. He was the first Armenian poet to transcribe his thoughts while in exile, but all that remain of his work are 17 poems and a handful of paintings based on books of the bible.

"Ghareeb" means a stranger or foreigner without property, money, or possessions; miserable, wretched. My own family name derives from this word.

"Strambotto": A Strambotto is a single stanza of eight, eleven-syllable lines, with the rhyme scheme ABABABAB. However, there are other forms: one consists of six lines; another of a different rhyme scheme than the ABABAB one.

"Fetish of Last Lines": Every line in this poem is the final line of a poem in my collection.

Acknowledgements

"Old Griefs" (in a very different form) was shortlisted for the *FreeFall* Poetry Contest and was published in *FreeFall*, Vol. XXV, No.2 (Spring/Summer 2015).

"Okra" was published in *Crave It* (Writers and Artists Do Food), edited by Kim Aubrey, Elaine Batcher, K.D. Miller, and Ruth Parker (Red Claw Press, 2011).

"Elegy" (as "Armenian Elegy") won First Prize in the 22nd Surrey International Writers Conference Poetry Contest, Vancouver, British Columbia, 2014.

"Sheep in Sun" won Honourable Mention in the 2015 William Henry Drummond Poetry Contest.

"A True Portrait of Talaat Pasha" was shortlisted as the Best Single Poem from a Suite in the Gwendolyn MacEwen/Exile Poetry Contest, 2015, and published in *Exile*, Vol. 40, No. 1.

"The Walls of Diyarbekir" was shortlisted for the 2015 GritLit Poetry Award and later published on Lola Koundakjian's Armenian Poetry Project website.

Barry Dempster, Allan Briesmaster, and David Scollard generously offered their time and comments on earlier versions of my manuscript. Bruce Meyer and Peter Balakian provided their expert editorial advice that helped improve many of the poems in general and the book's focus in particular.

Elana Wolff, my editor and long-time consulting poet, is owed a huge debt of gratitude for her continuing interest in and support of my work. Elana's rigorous yet sensitive editing has helped me chisel many of the poems to a nice, hard form.

Thanks, too, to Guernica Editions for an Ontario Writers Reserve Grant and to the Ontario Arts Council for the same.

I extend deep gratitude to my publishers Michael Mirolla and Connie McParland, and special thanks to Errol F. Richardson for the cover design.

About the Author

Keith Garebian is an award-winning author of sixteen books of non-fiction and now (with *Poetry is Blood*) seven of poetry. The recipient of the prestigious William Saroyan Medal (Armenia), he won a Canada Council grant to complete his authoritative biography of William Hutt, and numerous grants from the Ontario Arts Council, including two Work in Progress Grants (one for Prose, and one for Poetry). He has been published in over one hundred international newspapers, journals, magazines, and anthologies, and some of his work has been translated into French, German, Armenian, Chinese, Romanian, Bulgarian, and Hebrew. He has served on literary and theatre juries for the Ontario Arts Council, and his work has been referenced in more than fifty international books, articles, and theses. He posts reviews at www.stageandpage.com and "Garebian on the Arts" on Word Press. He also reviews books for *World Literature Today*.

Printed in February 2018
by Gauvin Press,
Gatineau, Québec